Two Israels Unveiled

Israel's Prophetic Journey, Volume 1

Michael Maher

Published by Michael Maher Ministries, 2024.

TWO ISRAELS UNVEILED

First edition. July 25, 2024.

ISBN: 979-8227475862

Written by Michael Maher.

Table of Contents

TWO ISRAELS UNVEILED

Michael E.B. Maher

Unless otherwise indicated, all Scripture quotations in this teaching are from the *New King James Version* of the bible.

2024

ISBN: 9798227475862

Books by Michael E.B. Maher

Foundation Doctrines of Christ

Repentance from Dead Works

Faith Toward God

Doctrine of Baptisms

Laying on of Hands

Resurrection of the Dead

Eternal Judgement

Man, the Image of God

The Will of Man

The Spirit of Man

The Conscience of Man

The Mind of Man

The Body of Man

Gifts of the Church

Spiritual Gifts

Ministry Gifts

The Revelation Gifts

The Power Gifts

The Speaking Gifts

Chapter 1

The Dual Israel Concept

Two Israel's: Unveiling Biblical Prophecy

Romans 9:6-8 but it is not that the word of God has taken no effect. For they are not all Israel who are of Israel, (7) nor are they all children because they are the seed of Abraham; but, "In Isaac, your seed shall be called." (8) That is, those who are the children of the flesh, these are not the children of God; but the children of the promise are counted as the seed.

The subject matter of this book is the first in a series that deals with biblical prophecy, specifically as it relates to the nation of Israel. For us to have a scriptural understanding of this particular subject, however, we need to recognize that scripture reveals to us that there are two Israel's. Sadly, because of their lack of understanding of this fundamental truth, many bible scholars misinterpret biblical prophecy in this area. And so the question is asked, with regards to bible prophecy, why is it important for us to understand the biblical truth about the two Israel's? The main reason is because both Israel's feature in bible prophecy; and what is prophesied about the one, invariably does not apply to the other, and visa versa. And so because most bible scholars acknowledge only one Israel, i.e. the nation of Israel; they therefore apply all bible prophecy to that Israel, thus creating a completely distorted picture about the future of that nation. An analogy that helps us to understand this concept would be the Jews acknowledging only one coming of the Messiah. Because Jews do not understand the biblical truth about the first and second coming of the Messiah, they therefore apply all biblical prophecy about the Messiah's coming to one event, thus creating a completely distorted picture about that event. So in this book, we want to discuss the biblical truth that there are two Israel's, and what the difference is between the two. The subject matter dealing with the two Israel's is substantial, and to do it justice requires a lot more detail than is recorded in this book. Nevertheless, in this book, I have dedicated three chapters to the subject, primarily so that we can correctly interpret bible prophecy pertaining specifically to the nation of Israel. In the above-quoted passage of scripture, the apostle Paul introduces us to the biblical truth that there are indeed two Israel's; for in this passage, he says that they are not all Israel who are of Israel. In other words, Paul is saying that not all the direct descendants of Israel (Jacob) are part of Israel. And so we see that even though all Israelis can prove, through their ancestry, that they are part of the nation of Israel; Paul speaks about another Israel, which to be considered part of, requires a qualification other than ancestry. Paul goes on in this passage to allude to the qualification required to be considered part of second Israel; i.e. being "children of the promise". And so having introduced the concept of the two Israel's in scripture, we will now explore that concept in more detail in this book. Let me say at the outset; that this teaching does not align with the unscriptural doctrine of "Replacement Theology". So what is Replacement Theology, or "Supersessionism" as it is also known? Briefly, the doctrine states that the church has replaced the nation of Israel as God's chosen people. In other words, this doctrine maintains that God has discarded the nation of Israel and the church has become the new Israel. Although there is an element of truth in this doctrine; because it only acknowledges one Israel, i.e. the church, it therefore applies all bible prophecy to that Israel, thus creating a completely distorted picture about the future of the church. The correct interpretation of scripture, however, teaches us that there are two Israel's; i.e. the church and the nation of Israel, and God has a separate plan for each one. As an aside, the two Israel's discussed in this book are not to be confused with the division of the nation of Israel into the two separate kingdoms, as recorded in the Old Testament; i.e. the Northern Kingdom of Israel and the Southern Kingdom of Judah. I discuss the subject of those two kingdoms in the next book in this series.

Chapter 2

5

Israel after the flesh

Physical Israel

1 Corinthians 10:16-18 The cup of blessing which we bless, is it not the communion of the blood of Christ? The bread which we break, is it not the communion of the body of Christ? (17) For we, though many, are one bread and one body; for we all partake of that one bread. (18) Observe Israel after the flesh: Are not those who eat of the sacrifices partakers of the altar?

In this chapter, we will discuss the first of the two Israel's. Let me say at the outset; that Israel which we will discuss in this chapter is the only one recognized in the world, and is the one most recognized in the church. In the above-quoted passage of scripture, the apostle Paul teaches the church the biblical truth, that when we partake of the bread and the wine, we have communion with the Lord Jesus Christ; i.e. we partake of that one bread, who is Christ. And so in trying to explain the concept of communion to us, Paul uses the Jewish priests as an illustration; for he says that when they eat of the sacrifices made on God's altar, they are partakers of the altar. For this discussion, however, the point I want to highlight from this passage is Paul's comment about Israel. Notice that Paul does not say, *"Observe Israel"*, but rather he says, *"Observe Israel after the flesh"*. So why does Paul make that distinction? He does so because he understands that there are two Israel's, and in this passage, he is alluding to one of them, i.e. Israel after the flesh. So what does Paul mean, when he makes the statement "Israel after the flesh"?

Romans 9:1-5 "I tell the truth in Christ, I am not lying, my conscience also bearing me witness in the Holy Spirit, (2) that I have great sorrow and continual grief in my heart. (3) For I could wish that I myself were accursed from Christ for my brethren, my countrymen according to the flesh, (4) who are Israelites, to whom pertain the adoption, the glory, the covenants, the giving of the law, the service of God, and the promises; (5) of whom are the fathers and from whom, according to the flesh, Christ came, who is over all, the eternally blessed God. Amen."

In the previous passage, Paul referred to "Israel after the flesh"; and we asked what he meant by that statement. In the above-quoted passage of scripture, Paul points us to the answer to that statement; for in this passage Paul speaks about his countrymen according to the flesh, "who are Israelites". And so clearly we can see from this passage that the term "Israel after the flesh", refers to those who are classified as Israelis or Jews. Although we will not discuss it at this time, Paul alludes to the second Israel in this passage; for he speaks of his "countrymen according to the flesh", thus implying that he has other "countrymen who are not according to the flesh".

Philippians 3:4-5 though I also might have confidence in the flesh. If anyone else thinks he may have confidence in the flesh, I more so: (5) circumcised the eighth day, of the stock of Israel, of the tribe of Benjamin, a Hebrew of the Hebrews; concerning the law, a Pharisee;

We have established thus far that "Israel after the flesh", refers to those who are classified as Israelis. The question is then asked, who qualifies to be an Israeli? The apostle Paul answers that question for us in the above-quoted passage of scripture; for in this passage, Paul lists the two criteria that qualified him as an Israeli (Hebrew). Paul lists the two criteria in order of importance; the first criterion was that he had been circumcised on the eighth day, and the second criterion was that he was of the stock of Israel and the tribe of Benjamin. We will first discuss the criterion of being of the stock of Israel. When Paul stated that he was of the stock of Israel and the tribe of Benjamin, he was saying that, because he could trace his ancestry back to Jacob (Israel) through the tribe of

Benjamin, he therefore qualified as an Israeli. That same principle applies to all Jews. And so we see that all Jews who can trace their ancestry back to Jacob, meet one of the two criteria to qualify as Israelis i.e. citizens of the nation of Israel.

Jacob: The Founder of Israel

Genesis 32:27-29 so He said to him, "What is your name?" He said, "Jacob." (28) And He said, "Your name shall no longer be called Jacob, but Israel; for you have struggled with God and with man, and have prevailed." (29) Then Jacob asked, saying, "Tell me Your name, I pray." And He said, "Why is it that you ask about My name?" And He blessed him there.

So why does Paul specifically mention in the previous passage, that he was from the stock of Israel? The reason is that God began the nation of Israel with Jacob as its founder. Jacob was the son of Isaac and grandson of Abraham. In the above-quoted passage of scripture we see that on the night that Jacob wrestled with the Lord, He changed Jacob's name to Israel. And so the nation of Israel took its name from its founder, Jacob. Scripture teaches us that Jacob had twelve sons, who in turn became the founders of the twelve tribes of Israel; i.e. Rueben, Simeon, Levi, Judah, Zebulun, Issachar, Dan, Gad, Asher, Naphtali, Joseph, and Benjamin (Genesis 49). And so the tribe of Benjamin, through which Paul could trace his ancestry, took its name from Jacob's youngest son. Therefore we can see that when Paul speaks of those who are "of Israel", he is referring to Jacob's biological descendants; i.e. Jews who can trace their ancestry back to Jacob as the father of the Israeli nation. As an aside, it is interesting to note that the Man that Jacob wrestled with that night was Christ, for the Lord says to Jacob that he had wrestled both with God and with Man; and it is Jesus Christ who is both God and Man. This highlights another truth which I will briefly mention now, and discuss in more detail later. In this passage, the Lord asks Jacob what his name is, to which Jacob replies "Jacob", and the Lord then changes Jacob's name to Israel. Jacob then asks the Lord what His name is, to which the Lord replies "Why do you ask about My name". The Lord's answer to Jacob's question seems a bit strange until we understand that Israel is the Lord's name. That particular truth explains why the Lord answered Jacob in that manner; for He was saying, why do you ask My name, I have just given it to you.

Genesis 16:15 So Hagar bore Abram a son; and Abram named his son, whom Hagar bore, Ishmael

Someone said, but surely the Jews can trace their ancestry back to Abraham. The Jews can certainly trace their ancestry back to Abraham, but they are not the only nation that can do that. In the above-quoted passage of scripture, we have the account of the birth of Abraham's first son, Ishmael. Biblical records reveal to us that Ishmael was the founder of the Ishmaelite people (Genesis 37:25); and it is widely accepted as a historical fact that the Arab nations today, are the biological descendants of the Ishmaelites[1]. And so we can see why being a biological descendant of Abraham does not qualify one to be an Israeli; because through Ishmael, the Arab nations are also the biological descendants of Abraham. This is one of the reasons why Jewish ancestry traced back to Jacob (Israel) is essential for one to qualify as an Israeli.

Genesis 17:3-5 Then Abram fell on his face, and God talked with him, saying: (4) "As for Me, behold, My covenant is with you, and you shall be a father of many nations. (5) No longer shall your name be called Abram, but your name shall be Abraham; for I have made you a father of many nations.

Abraham's first two sons (Abraham had numerous sons – Genesis 25) were Ishmael and Isaac. In the above-quoted passage of scripture we see that after Ishmael was born and before Isaac was born, God changed Abram's name to Abraham. And so technically speaking, it would be correct to say that the Arabs can trace their ancestry to "Abram" through Ishmael, whereas the Jews can trace their ancestry to "Abraham" through Isaac. Abraham's name change has a spiritual connotation to it, however, which does not impact the shared biological ancestry of both Jews and Arabs. An important point for us to note from this passage is that God made Abraham a father of not just one nation, but many nations; unlike Jacob, whom God made the father of just one nation i.e. the nation of Israel. Although we will not discuss it in this section, this particular truth about Abraham, alludes to the composition of the second Israel, i.e. it is made up of many nations. And so this is just another reason why Jewish ancestry traced back to Jacob (Israel) is essential for one to qualify as an Israeli.

Palestinian Ancestry: Esau's Descendants

Genesis 21:1-3 And the Lord visited Sarah as He had said, and the Lord did for Sarah as He had spoken. (2) For Sarah conceived and bore Abraham a son in his old age, at the set time of which God had spoken to him. (3) And Abraham called the name of his son who was born to him—whom Sarah bore to him—Isaac.

In the above-quoted passage of scripture, we have the account of Sarah giving birth to Isaac, the son whom she bore to Abraham in his old age. We have already mentioned that the reason why being a biological descendant of Abraham does not qualify one to be an Israeli is because the Arab nations are also the biological descendants of Abraham. So what about Abraham's son Isaac? Is it possible for the biological descendants of Isaac to be classified as Israelis; for surely the Jews can trace their ancestry back to Abraham's son Isaac through Isaac's son Jacob? The Jews can certainly trace their ancestry back to Isaac, but the problem is that Isaac had two sons, i.e. Esau and Jacob. And so the descendants of both sons can therefore trace their ancestry back to Isaac.

Genesis 25:21-26 Now Isaac pleaded with the Lord for his wife, because she was barren; and the Lord granted his plea, and Rebekah his wife conceived. (22) But the children struggled together within her; and she said, "If all is well, why am I like this?" So she went to inquire of the Lord. (23) And the Lord said to her: "Two nations are in your womb, two peoples shall be separated from your body; one people shall be stronger than the other, And the older shall serve the younger." (24) So when her days were fulfilled for her to give birth, indeed there were twins in her womb. (25) And the first came out red. He was like a hairy garment all over; so they called his name Esau. (26)

Afterward his brother came out, and his hand took hold of Esau's heel; so his name was called Jacob. Isaac was sixty years old when she bore them.

We have seen thus far that the Jews are Abraham's descendants through Isaac and Jacob, and the Arab nations are Abraham's descendants through Ishmael. And so the question is asked, which nation/people are Isaac's descendants through Esau? The answer to that question is that today's Palestinians are Isaac's biological descendants through Esau. Although it is widely understood that the Arab nations are the biological descendants of Ishmael, it is not widely understood that the Palestinians are the biological descendants of Esau. And so in light of that, we will now take a bit of time to establish this particular truth. Biblical records reveal to us that Esau was the founder of the Edomite nation (Genesis 36:9). And so we see that by identifying who the modern-day descendants of the Edomites are, we can therefore identify Esau's biological descendants. Historical records teach us that in the year 587 BC, after the conquest and exile of Judah by the Babylonians, the Edomites migrated to Judea and settled in the region of Hebron. The region of Hebron was vacant at the time because the Babylonians had forcefully expelled the Jews. Biblical records confirm this fact, for the Lord says of the Edomites, "Edom, who gave My land to themselves as a possession" (Ezekiel 36:5). As an aside, the Lord's comment to the Edomites in this passage is an ominous warning to their descendants that they are trespassing on His land. Nevertheless, the Edomites prospered in their new country for more than four centuries. Over time the geographic region of Judea fell first under Greek control, and then under the control of the Romans. During all this time the Edomites remained in the region around Hebron, and were called by the Greeks and Romans "Idumaea" or "Idumea". Around the time of Jesus, the Idumaeans constituted the majority of the population of Western Judea[2]. Biblical records confirm this because they speak of a great multitude from

Galilee, Judea, and Idumea coming to Jesus and following Him (Mark 3:7-8). The Idumaeans remained a significant and separate portion of the population of the Roman province of Judea, during both the first and second Jewish revolts against Rome, which took place in 70 and 136 AD respectively. The second Jewish revolt resulted in the final destruction of the Jewish population still living in Judea. It was at this time that the Roman province of Judea was renamed Syria Palaestina (i.e. Palestine). After the final expulsion of the Jews, a mixed population replaced them, made up of Roman veterans and immigrants from the neighbouring Roman provinces of Syria, Phoenicia, and Arabia[3]. Nevertheless, throughout this period the Idumaeans, who were the majority population, continued to reside in what had now become the Roman province of Syria Palaestina. The Roman Empire and its successor, the Byzantine Empire, continued to govern the province of Palestine until the year 637 AD. And so over time, all the inhabitants of Palestine (including the Idumaeans) eventually became known as Palestinians. In 637 AD, Palestine fell under Muslim control, and, other than a brief period between 1099 AD and 1291 AD when the Crusaders controlled Palestine, it remained under Muslim control for the next 1,300 years. It was during this period that nearly all Palestinians (including those of Idumaean descent) converted to Islam. That status quo remained in place until the year 1948 when the United Nations authorized the State of Israel to be established in the territory of Palestine. When that happened, a significant migration of Jews from around the world returned to settle in the newly created State of Israel. The local Palestinian population rejected the creation of the State of Israel on "their land" however, and a war broke out between the Jews and the Palestinians. The Palestinians lost the war, resulting in approximately 711,000 Palestinian refugees being displaced to three main locations, i.e. Gaza, the West Bank, and Jordan[4]. At the time of writing this book, approximately 5,500,000 Palestinians are living in the Israeli-occupied territories of the West Bank and the Gaza Strip[5], and a further 3,000,000 Palestinian refugees are living in Jordon[6]. And so we see that historical records show us that the people we know today as Palestinians, are the descendants of the Idumaeans/Edomites, who are the descendants of Esau. There is one further factor that shows that the Palestinians are Esau's descendants. Genetic studies have shown a close genetic relationship between Palestinians and Jews, suggesting a shared ancestral heritage[7]. Their shared ancestral heritage would be Isaac as the father of both Esau (the Palestinians) and Jacob (the Jews). And so when we add all of these factors together, we can very clearly see that the Palestinians are indeed Esau's descendants. As we will see later in this series, this particular truth will play a very significant role in the future of both the Israelis and Palestinians. Nevertheless, in this section, we want to concentrate on why Jewish ancestry must be traced back to Jacob. And so we see why being a biological descendant of Isaac cannot qualify one to be an Israeli; because through Esau, the Palestinian people are also the biological descendants of Isaac and Abraham. This is just another reason why Jewish ancestry traced back to Jacob (Israel) is essential for one to qualify as an Israeli. As an aside, the significance of the Palestinians living in Jordan is the fact that Mount Seir is located in Southern Jordan. So why is that significant? The reason is because scripture teaches us that God has given the territory of Mount Seir to Esau and his descendants (Deuteronomy 2:4-5). Therefore we can see that a significant portion of Esau's descendants (the 3,000,000 Palestinians living in Jordan) have finally returned to the land that the Lord originally gave them.

Circumcision and Citizenship: Israel's Qualification

Exodus 12:48-49 And when a stranger dwells with you and wants to keep the Passover to the Lord, let all his males be circumcised, and then let him come near and keep it; and he shall be as a native of the land. For no uncircumcised person shall eat it. (49) One law shall be for the native-born and for the stranger who dwells among you."

We have established thus far that someone who can trace their biological ancestry back to Jacob qualifies as a citizen of Israel. Nevertheless, there is another way for an individual to qualify as a citizen of Israel. In the above-quoted passage of scripture, God made provision for individuals who were not of Jewish descent (i.e. Gentiles), to become part of Israel if they so desired. The Lord said in this passage that those individuals would have to become circumcised. In other words, they would have to convert to Judaism, i.e. obey the Laws of Moses. The term applied to such individuals is "proselyte", and the Lord Jesus Himself acknowledged that such individuals were indeed part of the Jewish nation (Matthew 23:15).

Genesis 17:9-14 And God said to Abraham: "As for you, you shall keep My covenant, you and your descendants after you throughout their generations. (10) This is My covenant which you shall keep, between Me and you and your descendants after you: Every male child among you shall be circumcised; (11) and you shall be circumcised in the flesh of your foreskins, and it shall be a sign of the covenant between Me and you. (12) He who is eight days old among you shall be circumcised, every male child in your generations, he who is born in your house or bought with money from any foreigner who is not your descendant. (13) He who is born in your house and he who is bought with your money must be circumcised, and My covenant shall be in your flesh for an everlasting covenant. (14) And the uncircumcised male child, who is not circumcised in the flesh of his foreskin, that person shall be cut off from his people; he has broken My covenant."

In the previous passage we saw that through the act of circumcision, God made provision for Gentiles to become part of Israel, even though they are not Jacob's biological descendants. And so this brings us to the second criterion Paul mentioned, which qualifies an individual to be a citizen of Israel. The second criterion is that the individual must be circumcised. So why is circumcision a qualifying criterion for one to become part of Israel? In the above-quoted passage of scripture, we have an account of the covenant that God made with Abraham and his descendants, i.e. the nation of Israel. And so we see that the nation of Israel is unique among the nations of the world because they have a covenant relationship with God. God stated in this passage that the sign of His covenant was that every male descended from Abraham had to be circumcised in the flesh of their foreskins, eight days after birth. And so we see the reason for circumcision; it identifies the individual as being a partaker of God's covenant with the nation of Israel. God went on to say in this passage that any descendant of Abraham who is not circumcised, has broken His covenant and would be cut off from His people. In other words, in God's eyes, they are no longer considered part of the nation of Israel. And so we can see two reasons why, in determining whether one is a citizen of Israel or not, the qualifying criterion of circumcision is ranked above ancestry; firstly, because it is possible for an individual not of Jewish descent, to become circumcised and thus part of Israel, and secondly because an individual of Jewish decent can be cut off from Israel by breaking God's covenant of circumcision.

Circumcision: Key to Hebrew Identity

Genesis 17:18-27 And Abraham said to God, "Oh, that Ishmael might live before You!" (19) Then God said: "No, Sarah your wife shall bear you a son, and you shall call his name Isaac; I will establish My covenant with him for an everlasting covenant, and with his descendants after him. (20) And as for Ishmael, I have heard you. Behold, I have blessed him and will make him fruitful, and will multiply him exceedingly. He shall beget twelve princes, and I will make him a great nation. (21) But My covenant I will establish with Isaac, whom Sarah shall bear to you at this set time next year." (22) Then He finished talking with him, and God went up from Abraham. (23) So Abraham took Ishmael his son, all who were born in his house and all who were bought with his money, every male among the men of Abraham's house, and circumcised the flesh of their foreskins that very same day, as God had said to him. (24) Abraham was ninety-nine years old when he was circumcised in the flesh of his foreskin. (25) And Ishmael his son was thirteen years old when he was circumcised in the flesh of his foreskin. (26) That very same day Abraham was circumcised, and his son Ishmael; (27) and all the men of his house, born in the house or bought with money from a foreigner, were circumcised with him.

We have established thus far that circumcision is the more important criterion for qualifying an individual to be part of the Hebrew nation; and in the above-quoted passage of scripture we see that on the day that God gave Abraham the covenant of circumcision, Abraham circumcised his son Ishmael. And so the question is asked, as one who was circumcised, was Ishmael included in God's covenant with Israel? The answer to that question is that it depends on which Israel you are referring to. I do not doubt that Ishmael was included in second Israel (which we will discuss in the next chapter), for the scriptures teach us that when Ishmael died, he was gathered to his people (Genesis 25:17). The scriptures only speak of the death of the saints in this manner; for example, when Abraham (Genesis 25:8), Isaac (Genesis 35:29) and Jacob (Genesis 49:33) died, the scripture says that they were gathered to their people. Nevertheless, even though Ishmael was part of the Israel of God, he was not part of Israel after the flesh, and therefore he was not included in the Covenant of circumcision that God made with the nation of Israel. That particular truth is revealed to us in this passage, for the Lord specifically states that His covenant of circumcision was not with Ishmael, but rather with Isaac. We have seen earlier, that the Arab nations are the descendants of Ishmael, and it is common knowledge that the Arab nations practice circumcision. And so the question is asked, if Ishmael and his descendants are not included in God's covenant of circumcision, why do the Arab nations practice circumcision? Obviously, Ishmael passed on to his descendants the practice of circumcision; and so when the Arab nations embraced the Muslim faith approximately 2,500 years later, their inherited practice of circumcision became part of the Muslim faith. Historical records confirm this, because according to historians of religion and scholars of Religious studies, the Islamic tradition of circumcision was derived from the Pagan practices and rituals of pre-Islamic Arabia,and is never mentioned in the Quran[8]. Nevertheless, even though the Arab (and all Muslim) nations practice circumcision, they are not included in God's covenant of circumcision with the nation of Israel. This point highlights the fact that circumcision alone does not qualify one to become part of the nation of Israel, but rather conversion to Judaism.

Esau: Birthright and Covenant

Romans 9:9-13 for this is the word of promise: "At this time I will come and Sarah shall have a son." (10) And not only this, but when Rebecca also had conceived by one man, even by our father Isaac (11) (for the children not yet being born, nor having done any good or evil, that the purpose of God according to election might stand, not of works but of Him who calls), (12) it was said to her, "The older shall serve the younger." (13) As it is written, "Jacob I have loved, but Esau I have hated."

We have established thus far that even though Ishmael was circumcised and his descendants practiced circumcision, nevertheless they were not included in God's covenant of circumcision; because they had not converted to Judaism. And so this brings us to Esau and his descendants. We have seen in the previous passage that God established His covenant of circumcision with Isaac, and Isaac would have circumcised both Esau and Jacob on the eighth day after their birth. And so according to the scriptures that we have seen in this chapter thus far; as direct descendants of both Abraham and Isaac and also being circumcised on the eighth day, both Esau and Jacob would have been included in God's covenant of circumcision. And yet we have the account in the scripture quoted above where God says, "Jacob I have loved, but Esau I have hated". Clearly, as one whom the Lord hates, Esau reached a point when he broke God's covenant and was therefore cut off from His people (Genesis 17:14). And so the question is asked, what did Esau do to elicit this response from the Lord?

Hebrews 12:14-17 Pursue peace with all people, and holiness, without which no one will see the Lord: (15) looking carefully lest anyone fall short of the grace of God; lest any root of bitterness springing up cause trouble, and by this many become defiled; (16) lest there be any fornicator or profane person like Esau, who for one morsel of food sold his birthright. (17) For you know that afterward when he wanted to inherit the blessing, he was rejected, for he found no place for repentance, though he sought it diligently with tears.

We have asked the question, what did Esau do that caused him to be cut off from God's covenant of circumcision? The apostle Paul provides us with the answer in the above-quoted passage of scripture; for in this passage, Paul teaches us that the Lord rejected Esau because he sold his birthright. Paul goes on to tell us in this passage that when Esau finally realized the full impact of his action, he diligently and tearfully sought repentance for what he had done, nevertheless there was no recourse. The full account of Esau's attempted repentance is recorded in the book of Genesis 27:30-38.

Genesis 25:29-34 Now Jacob cooked a stew; and Esau came in from the field, and he was weary. (30) And Esau said to Jacob, "Please feed me with that same red stew, for I am weary." Therefore his name was called Edom. (31) But Jacob said, "Sell me your birthright as of this day." (32) And Esau said, "Look, I am about to die; so what is this birthright to me?" (33) Then Jacob said, "Swear to me as of this day." So he swore to him and sold his birthright to Jacob. (34) And Jacob gave Esau bread and stew of lentils; then he ate and drank, arose, and went his way. Thus Esau despised his birthright.

The incident of Esau selling his birthright is recorded in the above-quoted passage of scripture. This passage declares that Esau despised his birthright, and that would be an accurate description of Esau's attitude; because to sell one's birthright for a plate of food after a hard day's work, was a display of Esau's utter contempt for his birthright as Isaac's firstborn son. And so many years later, because of what Esau had done, God allowed Jacob to deceive Isaac into bestowing Esau's blessing upon Jacob. The account of that incident, including God's prophetic words spoken over both Jacob and Esau's descendants on that occasion, is recorded in Genesis 27. Because the prophetic words spoken by Isaac on that occasion impacted the futures of both the Jews and the Palestinians, we will discuss them later in this series. Nevertheless, in this section, we want to concentrate on the reason why Esau and his descendants are excluded from God's covenant of circumcision. And so in light of that, the question is asked, why was Esau's despising of his birthright so significant, that it elicited God's response of cutting Esau off from His covenant? The answer lies in Esau's right as Isaac's firstborn son. So what right was that? We have seen in an earlier passage that God changed Jacob's name to Israel, thus making him the father of the nation of Israel (Genesis 32:28). And so as Isaac's firstborn son, it was Esau's right to have his name changed to Israel, and thus become the father of the nation of Israel. So how do we know that? For us to understand that concept we need to recognize that just as the Old Covenant is a copy and shadow of the New Covenant (Hebrews 8:4-13), Israel after the flesh is a copy and shadow of the Israel of God. So why is it important for us, in this context, to understand that Israel after the flesh is the shadow of the Israel of God? The reason is because of who the Father of the Israel of God is; it is the Lord Jesus Christ. We know that because God said it was; *"Then you shall say to Pharaoh, 'Thus says the Lord: "Israel is My son, My firstborn"* (Exodus 4:22). And so we see that when Esau rejected his birthright to be named the father of Israel after the flesh, he was rejecting the Father of the Israel of God, i.e. Jesus (Israel) the Messiah, God's firstborn Son. Understanding this truth explains why Esau's despising of his birthright, was the cause of his being cut off from God's covenant of circumcision. Because this particular truth pertains to the second Israel, we will discuss this concept in a lot more detail in the following chapter. When Esau was cut off from God's covenant, it impacted his descendants as well; for unlike Ishmael, Esau never passed on to his descendants the practice of circumcision. We know that because historical records reveal to us that in the year 110 BC, the Jews attempted to force some of the Idumaeans living in Judea to convert to Judaism. Before the Idumaeans could convert however, they first had to be circumcised, thus indicating that unlike Ishmael's descendants, circumcision was not practiced by Esau's descendants[9]. And so we see that God's promise to Abraham applied to Esau's descendants, i.e. those who were not circumcised would be cut off from His people and His covenant. Many centuries later when the Idumaeans, as part of the Palestinian population, converted to the Muslim faith, they then also adopted the Muslim tradition of circumcision. Nevertheless, even though the Palestinians practice circumcision, they are not included in God's covenant of circumcision with the nation of Israel. And so we have seen in this chapter that the first Israel is referred to in scripture, as Israel after the flesh. And we have seen that there are two criteria for one to qualify as a member of the nation of Israel. Firstly, one must be a partaker of God's covenant of circumcision with the nation of Israel, i.e. one must be part of the Jewish faith. And secondly, one must be a biological descendant of Jacob, the founder of the nation of Israel.

Temporal Nature of Israel

Hebrews 8:13 In that He says, "A New Covenant," He has made the first obsolete. Now what is becoming obsolete and growing old is ready to vanish away.

There is one last point that needs to be mentioned about Israel after the flesh; which is its longevity. So what do I mean by that statement? I have already mentioned that just as the Old Covenant is a shadow of the New Covenant, Israel after the flesh is also a shadow of the Israel of God. And so in light of that truth, we have the above-quoted passage of scripture where the apostle Paul compares the Old Covenant with the New Covenant. And in this passage, Paul says of the Old Covenant, that it is becoming obsolete and growing old and is ready to vanish away. In the same manner Israel after the flesh is also ready to vanish away. So what do I mean by that statement? When the Old Covenant finally ends at the end of the age, Israel after the flesh will also cease to exist with it. From that point on, only the New Covenant and the Israel of God will remain; i.e. there will no longer be two Covenants and two Israel's. And so we see that because Israel after the flesh will cease to exist at the end of the age, that indicates to us that God's purposes for the first Israel will come to an end at the end of this current age. In other words, God's purpose for Israel after the flesh is temporary and not eternal.

Chapter 3

27

Israel of God

28

The Church: The Second Israel

Galatians 6:12-16 As many as desire to make a good showing in the flesh, these would compel you to be circumcised, only that they may not suffer persecution for the cross of Christ. (13) For not even those who are circumcised keep the law, but they desire to have you circumcised that they may boast in your flesh. (14) But God forbid that I should boast except in the cross of our Lord Jesus Christ, by whom the world has been crucified to me, and I to the world. (15) For in Christ Jesus neither circumcision nor uncircumcision avails anything, but a new creation. (16) And as many as walk according to this rule, peace and mercy be upon them, and upon the Israel of God.

In this chapter, we will discuss the second of the two Israel's. The Israel that we will discuss in this chapter, the world knows nothing about, and most of the church falls into that same category, i.e. they know little or nothing about the second Israel. This particular truth is extremely ironic because as we will see in this chapter, it is the church that is the second Israel. In the above-quoted passage of scripture, the apostle Paul introduces us to the second Israel. The context of this passage is that false Jewish "ministers of the gospel" had gone to the Gentile churches in Galatia, and were trying to convince them that unless they were circumcised and kept the Law of Moses, they could not be saved. The message of "salvation" which they proclaimed was that believing that Jesus died on the cross for our sins was not enough, for one also had to become part of the nation of Israel to be saved. In other words, one had to convert to Judaism. These Jewish "ministers" put themselves forward as examples, proclaiming that they also "believed" that Jesus died on the cross for their sins; nevertheless, it was because they were Jews, and therefore part of Israel, that they were saved. And so in response to the false gospel proclaimed by these Jewish "ministers", Paul warned the

Galatian churches not to be deceived; for nothing other than faith in the cross of the Lord Jesus, is required to be saved. Paul then goes on in this passage to teach the church, that in Christ Jesus neither circumcision nor uncircumcision avails anything, but a new creation. So what does that statement mean? The "circumcision" in this passage refers to Jews (Israel after the flesh). The "uncircumcision" in this passage refers to Gentiles. The "new creation" in this passage refers to the spirits of believers that become new creations in Christ Jesus when they are born again (2 Corinthians 5:17). And so Paul teaches us in this passage that neither being a Jew nor being a Gentile means anything in Christ Jesus, but rather it is the born again spirit that matters. Paul goes on in this passage to commend believers who understand this principle and walk according to it, and then Paul introduces us to the second Israel; for he refers to these believers as being "the Israel of God". And so we see that Paul teaches us that there are two Israel's, for he refers to the one as the "circumcision" and he refers to the other as "a new creation". The circumcision in this passage refers to Israel after the flesh, for it is in the flesh that Jews are circumcised. The new creation in this passage refers to the Israel of God, for it is in the spirit that the saints are born again to become new creations in Christ Jesus. And so we see that being part of "Israel after the flesh" has nothing to do with being part of "the Israel of God"; for the qualifications required for being part of the first Israel differs from the qualifications required for being part of the second Israel. One must be circumcised to become part of Israel after the flesh, and one must be born again to become part of the Israel of God, and neither qualification pertains to the other. In other words, being circumcised does not qualify one to be part of the Israel of God, and being born again does not qualify one to be part of Israel after the flesh. Someone will say, but surely Jews (circumcision) can become part of the Israel of God if they become born again. That is indeed correct, and the apostle Paul is a classic example of that exact scenario. Nevertheless, Paul did not gain access to the Israel of God because he was circumcised, but rather because he was born again. And so we see that Jews that are born again fall into a unique category, for they become part of both Israel's, i.e. Israel after the flesh, and the Israel of God.

As an aside, this particular truth tends to become a stumbling block among certain sects in the church. So why do I say that? Compared to Gentile believers, Jewish believers are under a different dispensation of grace; which is why Paul differentiates between the gospel to the circumcised and the gospel to the uncircumcised (Galatians 2:7). So what dispensation of grace am I referring to? Before Jewish believers become partakers of the New Covenant, they are already partakers of the Old Covenant. In other words, they come from a background of already having a covenant relationship with God. And so God gives them grace to continue the practices they have learnt under the Old Covenant; until they mature enough to understand how to walk in the New Covenant. When certain sects of Gentile believers observe Jewish believers practicing the Laws of Moses, they erroneously assume that God allows/requires all believers to observe those same Laws. What those Gentile believers fail to understand, however, is that they come from a background of having no covenant relationship with God, i.e. they were never partakers of the Old Covenant. And so Gentile believers have no need of God's grace in this area, and none is given. Therefore when Gentile believers attempt to observe the Laws of Moses, they step outside of their dispensation of grace and place themselves under law. Paul warns Gentile believers from going down this path, because it leads to eventual separation from Christ (Galatians 5:4). In other words, Gentile believers who choose to become part of Israel after the flesh (i.e. become circumcised), cut themselves off from being part of the Israel of God. And so we see that, unlike their Jewish brethren; it is impossible for Gentile believers to become part of both Israel's. Someone will say, but does that mean that God favours Jewish believers over Gentile believers? The answer to that question is emphatically no, for God shows personal favouritism to no man (Galatians 2:6). However, explaining this particular concept requires far more detail than the scope of this book allows. I discuss this concept in more detail in my book "The Two Gospels Explained".

> *Romans 2:17-29 Indeed you are called a Jew, and rest on the law, and make your boast in God, (18) and know His will, and approve the things that are excellent, being instructed out of the law, (19) and are confident that you yourself are a guide to the blind, a light to those who are in darkness, (20) an instructor of the foolish, a teacher of babes, having the form of knowledge and truth in the law. (21) You, therefore, who teach another, do you not teach yourself? You who preach that a man should not steal, do you steal? (22) You who say, "Do not commit adultery," do you commit adultery? You who abhor idols, do you rob temples? (23) You who make your boast in the law, do you dishonour God through breaking the law? (24) For "The name of God is blasphemed among the Gentiles because of you," as it is written. (25) For circumcision is indeed profitable if you keep the law; but if you are a breaker of the law, your circumcision has become uncircumcision. (26) Therefore, if an uncircumcised man keeps the righteous requirements of the law, will not his uncircumcision be counted as circumcision? (27) And will not the physically uncircumcised, if he fulfils the law, judge you who, even with your written code and circumcision, are a transgressor of the law? (28) For he is not a Jew who is one outwardly, nor is circumcision that which is outward in the flesh; (29) but he is a Jew who is one inwardly; and circumcision is that of the heart, in the Spirit, not in the letter; whose praise is not from men but from God.*

We have seen in the previous passage that the apostle Paul introduced us to the concept of a second Israel; which he called the Israel of God. And so we see that there are two Israel's. The first Israel is referred to as

Israel after the flesh, and we have seen that one becomes a member of that Israel through circumcision and ancestry. The second Israel is referred to as the Israel of God, and we have seen that one becomes a member of that Israel through the new birth. In the above-quoted passage of scripture, the apostle Paul again reinforces the scriptural truth about the two Israel's. Although Paul does not speak specifically about two Israel's in this passage, he does, however, speak about two types of Jews. However, being a Jew and being an Israelite is the same thing, and so the concept remains the same; i.e. two types of Jews is the same as having two Israel's. The context of this passage is that Paul was destroying the argument that Jews (after the flesh) put forward; that their status before God is secure, simply because they are Jews. In other words, because they are God's chosen people. Paul exposes the hypocrisy of their argument, by showing the Jews, that when they proclaim that they are God's chosen people, their wicked behaviour blasphemes the name of God among the nations of the world. With regards to the two Israel's, Paul confirms in this passage that being a Jew outwardly in the flesh (circumcised in the flesh) qualifies one to be part of Israel after the flesh, whereas being a Jew inwardly in the spirit (circumcised in the spirit) qualifies one to be part of the Israel of God. Paul takes the argument even further because he teaches us in this passage that ultimately it is only those who belong to the Israel of God that are the real Jews, and those who belong to Israel after the flesh and call themselves Jews, are not real Jews; for Paul says in this passage that a Jew is not one outwardly in the flesh, but rather a Jew is one inwardly in the spirit. The Lord Jesus Himself concurs with the apostle Paul on this issue; for the Lord tells us that even though Israelis say they are Jews, they are actually lying; because as far as heaven is concerned, they aren't Jews at all (Revelation 3:9). And so the question is asked, are the Lord Jesus and the apostle Paul saying that Israel after the flesh no longer exists, and has been replaced with the Israel of God? Not at all; they are simply reaffirming the spiritual truth which I mentioned earlier; i.e. that Israel after the flesh is merely the shadow of the true Israel, i.e. the Israel of God.

> *Romans 9:1-9 "I tell the truth in Christ, I am not lying, my conscience also bearing me witness in the Holy Spirit, (2) that I have great sorrow and continual grief in my heart. (3) For I could wish that I myself were accursed from Christ for my brethren, my countrymen according to the flesh, (4) who are Israelites, to whom pertain the adoption, the glory, the covenants, the giving of the law, the service of God, and the promises; (5) of whom are the fathers and from whom, according to the flesh, Christ came, who is over all, the eternally blessed God. Amen. (6) But it is not that the word of God has taken no effect. For they are not all Israel who are of Israel, (7) nor are they all children because they are the seed of Abraham; but, "In Isaac, your seed shall be called." (8) That is, those who are the children of the flesh, these are not the children of God; but the children of the promise are counted as the seed. (9) For this is the word of promise: "At this time I will come and Sarah shall have a son."*

We have seen in the previous passage that the apostle Paul differentiated between Jews in the flesh and Jews in the spirit, thus confirming the spiritual truth that there are two Israel's. In the above-quoted passage of scripture, Paul once again reaffirms the truth that there are indeed two Israel's; for in this passage, Paul states that they are not all Israel who are of Israel. And so we see that the two Israel's which Paul mentions in this passage are; firstly those who "are Israel", and secondly those who are "of Israel". So what is the difference between the two? Paul tells us in this passage that those who "are Israel" are the children of God, and those who are "of Israel" are children of the flesh. Paul elaborates further, by telling us that the children of the flesh refer to those who are the biological descendants of Abraham through Jacob (Israel); and the children of God refer to those who, as the children of promise, are counted as the seed. Paul also teaches us in this passage that the children of the flesh do not qualify as the children of God, for it is only the children of the promise that are counted as the seed. In other words, it is only the children of the promise that are counted as the children of God. The children of the flesh in this passage refer to Israel after the flesh, and the children of God in this passage refer to the Israel of God.

> *Galatians 3:16 Now to Abraham and his Seed were the promises made. He does not say, "And to seeds," as of many, but as of one, "And to your Seed," who is Christ.*

We have seen in the previous passage that the apostle Paul stated that the children of promise are counted as the seed, i.e. they are the children of God. Paul teaches us in that passage that the seed he is referring to is not the biological descendants of Abraham (Israel after the flesh); for God told Abraham that in Isaac his seed would be called. And so the question is asked, what seed is Paul referring to? Paul answers that question for us in the above-quoted passage of scripture; for he tells us that the seed to whom the promises of God were made, is Christ. And so we see that the children of God are the children of Christ. It would be more accurate to say that the children of God are part of Christ; for scripture teaches us that all believers are baptized into Christ as sons of God (Galatians 3:26-27). And so we see that the Israel of God refers to all believers who have been baptized into Christ.

Jesus: Founder of Israel

Exodus 4:21-23 And the Lord said to Moses, "When you go back to Egypt, see that you do all those wonders before Pharaoh which I have put in your hand. But I will harden his heart so that he will not let the people go. (22) Then you shall say to Pharaoh, 'thus says the Lord: "Israel is My son, My firstborn. (23) So I say to you, let My son go that he may serve Me. But if you refuse to let him go, indeed I will kill your son, your firstborn."'"

In the previous chapter where we discussed Israel after the flesh, we saw that God changed Jacob's name to Israel, thus making him the father of the nation of Israel. In other words, the nation of Israel took its name from its founder. So what about the Israel of God? In other words, who is the Founder of the Israel of God? The above-quoted passage of scripture answers that question for us. The context of this passage is that God was instructing Moses what to say to Pharaoh when he approached him to let the people of Israel go out of Egypt. God's specific words to Pharaoh were, *"Israel is My son, My firstborn. So I say to you, let My son go that he may serve Me"*. It is important to note that God does not speak about the descendants of Israel in this instance, but rather He specifically names Israel, and He calls Him His firstborn Son. Although Jacob was the founder of the nation of Israel, he was never God's firstborn Son. And so we see that God was not referring to Jacob in this instance, but rather He was referring to the one who gave Jacob his name; the one that scripture reveals as being the firstborn Son of God, i.e. the Lord Jesus Christ (Romans 8:29). So why does God say in this passage, "Let My Son go that He may serve Me", instead of saying "let My people go that they may serve Me"? The reason is that God is not speaking about Israel after the flesh in this instance, but rather He is speaking about the Israel of God; i.e. the believing Jews who were part of Christ (Israel).

And so in that context, God correctly speaks about Israel (Christ) His Son. We know that God is speaking about the Lord Jesus in this instance because He says to Pharaoh that if he refused to let His Son go free, God would kill Pharaoh's firstborn son. God could legally do that because many centuries later His own firstborn Son would be killed as a ransom for the Israel of God (Mark 10:45). And so we see that Israel is the name of the Lord Jesus Christ, and the Israel of God takes its name from its Father, the Lord Jesus Christ.

> *Hosea 11:1 "When Israel was a child, I loved him, and out of Egypt I called My son.*

> *Matthew 2:13-15 Now when they had departed, behold, an angel of the Lord appeared to Joseph in a dream, saying, "Arise, take the young Child and His mother, flee to Egypt, and stay there until I bring you word; for Herod will seek the young Child to destroy Him." (14) When he arose, he took the young Child and His mother by night and departed for Egypt, (15) and was there until the death of Herod that it might be fulfilled which was spoken by the Lord through the prophet, saying, "Out of Egypt I called My Son."*

The above-quoted passages of scripture confirm the truth that Israel is one of the names given to the Lord Jesus Christ. In the first passage, God names His Son Israel, for He says, *"When Israel was a child, I loved him, and out of Egypt I called My son"*. We know that God was referring to the Lord Jesus Christ in Hosea's prophecy, because in the second passage, Matthew quotes Hosea's prophecy as being fulfilled in the childhood of the Lord Jesus. And so these passages teach us that Israel is one of the names given to the Lord Jesus Christ. I have stated earlier that Israel after the flesh is the shadow of the Israel of God. That same truth applies to the name given to Israel after the flesh, for it was Israel Himself (Jesus Christ) who changed Jacob's name to Israel. In other words, Israel (Jesus) gave Jacob His name. And so we see that Israel after the flesh ultimately gets its name from the Israel of God.

The Church: Twelve Tribes Scattered

James 1:1 James, a bondservant of God and of the Lord Jesus Christ, to the twelve tribes which are scattered abroad: Greetings.

We have already mentioned that Israel after the flesh is the shadow of the Israel of God. We have also seen in the previous section that God divided the nation of Israel into twelve tribes founded by the twelve sons of Jacob. And so we see that God did that to mirror the twelve tribes that constitute the Israel of God. The apostle James confirms that truth for us in the above-quoted passage of scripture, for in this passage James is not writing to the Jewish nation, he is writing to the church; and in doing so, he refers to the church as the twelve tribes which are scattered abroad. And so we see two truths revealed to us in this passage. Firstly, we see that the Israel of God, which includes both Jewish and Gentile believers, is made up of twelve tribes. Secondly, we see that God views His saints as being scattered abroad throughout the earth.

1 Peter 1:1-2 Peter, an apostle of Jesus Christ, To the pilgrims of the Dispersion in Pontus, Galatia, Cappadocia, Asia, and Bithynia, (2) elect according to the foreknowledge of God the Father, in sanctification of the Spirit, for obedience and sprinkling of the blood of Jesus Christ: Grace to you and peace be multiplied.

We have seen in the previous passage that the apostle James referred to the church as the twelve tribes which are scattered abroad. In the above-quoted passage of scripture, we see that the apostle Peter concurs with James' statement, for in this passage, Peter is not writing to the Jewish nation, he is also writing to the church; and in doing so, he refers to the church as the pilgrims of the Dispersion. So what does that statement mean? When the Lord refers to His saints as pilgrims, He is confirming the truth that this world is not our home and that we are just pilgrims who are passing through. So why does the Lord refer to His saints as the Dispersion in this passage? The answer to that question is given to us when we look at Israel after the flesh; for the term "Dispersion" is used to describe Jews who live outside of their God-given homeland, i.e. the land of Israel (John 7:35). And so we see that the Jewish nation mirrors the Israel of God in this area as well, for the term "Dispersion" describes the saints on earth living outside of their God-given homeland, i.e. the new Jerusalem (Revelation 21:1-3). And so we see that both James and Peter refer to the church as being scattered/dispersed throughout the earth.

God's Second Gathering Explained

Isaiah 11:9-16 They shall not hurt nor destroy in all My holy mountain, For the earth shall be full of the knowledge of the Lord As the waters cover the sea. (10) "And in that day there shall be a Root of Jesse, Who shall stand as a banner to the people; for the Gentiles shall seek Him, and His resting place shall be glorious." (11) It shall come to pass in that day That the Lord shall set His hand again the second time To recover the remnant of His people who are left, From Assyria and Egypt, From Pathros and Cush, From Elam and Shinar, From Hamath and the islands of the sea. (12) He will set up a banner for the nations and will assemble the outcasts of Israel, and gather together the dispersed of Judah from the four corners of the earth. (13) Also the envy of Ephraim shall depart, and the adversaries of Judah shall be cut off; Ephraim shall not envy Judah, and Judah shall not harass Ephraim. (14) But they shall fly down upon the shoulder of the Philistines toward the west; together they shall plunder the people of the East; they shall lay their hand on Edom and Moab; and the people of Ammon shall obey them. (15) The Lord will utterly destroy the tongue of the Sea of Egypt; With His mighty wind, He will shake His fist over the River, and strike it in the seven streams, and make men cross over dry-shod. (16) There will be a highway for the remnant of His people who will be left from Assyria, as it was for Israel in the day that he came up from the land of Egypt.

In the previous passages, we established that the Israel of God is referred to as being scattered/dispersed throughout the earth. This particular truth helps us to correctly interpret prophetic scripture dealing with the recovery of the remnant of God's people for example. The above-quoted passage of scripture is a case in point; for it refers to the Lord recovering the remnant of His people throughout the earth. In this passage the Lord specifically refers to a second time that He will do this, thus implying that there are two gatherings of the remnant of His people. Because they only recognize one Israel, many bible scholars interpret this passage to mean that God's first recovery of the remnant of His people took place when the Jews returned from Babylonian captivity in the year 539 BC, and the second recovery of the remnant of His people began when the Jews started to return to the newly created State of Israel in the year 1948. However, because this passage also refers to the various nations of the earth obeying the remnant of God's people, these various bible scholars are therefore forced to create an unscriptural dispensation, during which the nation of Israel will govern the earth. Because the subject matter of this series deals primarily with the nation of Israel, we will discuss both the 539 BC and 1948 AD events in detail, and what we will see is that the first recovery refers to the 1948 event, not the 539 BC event, thus indicating that the second recovery event has not yet taken place. That particular truth aligns with the context of the above-quoted passage of scripture, which deals specifically with the second coming of the Lord Jesus and His gathering together of the church (the Israel of God). In other words, it has nothing to do with the nation of Israel; and so because we have established the truth of two Israel's, we can therefore correctly interpret this passage of scripture to show that the second recovery event refers to Israel of God and not Israel after the flesh.

And so in this chapter, we have established that the second Israel is called the Israel of God. We have also seen that there is one criterion for qualifying as a member of the Israel of God, i.e. one must be born again. We have also seen that the Israel of God takes its name from its founder, the Lord Jesus Christ, whom God also names Israel. We have also seen in this section that the Israel of God consists of twelve tribes that are scattered throughout the earth. We have also seen in the previous chapter that the Israel of God is the eternal Israel, whereas Israel after the flesh will be done away with at the end of this current age.

We have also mentioned that Israel after the flesh is the shadow of the Israel of God, and we need to keep that point in mind as we examine prophetic scripture about Israel. And so I have used this book to establish the biblical truth that there are two Israel's, i.e. Israel after the flesh and the Israel of God. The reason I did that was so that we could correctly interpret prophetic scripture concerning the nation of Israel, which is the focus of this series. Therefore, other than this book, we will not have any further discussions in this series about prophetic scripture about the Israel of God (the church), for that is a subject requiring a book/series of its own.

If you believe you can receive Jesus as your Lord and Saviour by praying this prayer

Dear Heavenly Father,

I come to You in the Name of Jesus.

Your Word says, "the one who comes to Me I will by no means cast out" (John 6:37), so I know You won't cast me out, but You take me in and I thank You for it. You said in Your Word, "Whoever calls on the name of the Lord shall be saved." (Romans 10:13). I am calling on Your Name, so I know that You save me right now. You also said, "If you confess with your mouth the Lord Jesus and believe in your heart that God has raised Him from the dead, you will be saved. (10) For with the heart one believes unto righteousness, and with the mouth confession is made unto salvation" (Romans 10:9-10). I believe in my heart Jesus Christ is the Son of God. I believe that He was raised from the dead for my justification, and I confess Him now as my Lord. Because Your Word says, "with the heart one believes unto righteousness," and I do believe with my heart, I have now become the righteousness of God in Christ Jesus (2 Cor. 5:21) ...

And I am now saved!

Thank You, Lord!

Welcome to the family of God. Now that you are His child you need to read your bible (especially the New Testament) daily, spend time in prayer daily and join a local church that will teach you to be filled with the Holy Spirit with the evidence of speaking in other tongues, so that you can grow spiritually. You also need to tell others how Jesus has saved you so that they too can be saved.

About the Author

From childhood, Michael E.B. Maher has always known that the Lord's call was upon his life for the ministry. When he was saved at the age of twenty-two, almost immediately the Lord Jesus began to deal with him about entering the ministry. However, it was only many years latter that he committed to the Lord to answer the Lord's call to the ministry. And so, in 2014 Michael Maher Ministries was begun. From the beginning, the mandate given to Michael from the Lord Jesus was to preach the word. And so, this ministry preaches the word of God on every available platform around the world.

Michael Maher Ministries

Free Subscription

Join hundreds of others from countries around the world and read our Daily Bible Teaching Email and more, that will help you to grow in your walk with the Lord Jesus.

Thank you, sir, for helping me to understand these teachings clearly! Amen

> *- Tawanda Masvina*

Amen to keeping on keeping on. Thank you for today's lesson. We must never forget to pray regularly and immerse ourselves in the Word – "a page (or Chapter) a day helps keep Satan at bay".

Blessings,

> *- John Lombard*

Thank you so much for today's inspiration. This made so much sense to me and helped me overcome a huge block in my understanding.

Blessings and love

> *- Pam Laughton*

Log on to our website to subscribe.

www.mebmaher.wixsite.com/website[1]

---

1. http://www.mebmaher.wixsite.com/website

Michael Maher Ministries

Online Bible Courses

Our courses are designed to help believers grow in their faith and reach their full potential in Christ that God intended for their lives, through the study of His word.

Flexible

Enrol any time: choose your topic of study; study at your own pace.

Affordable

Pay as you go.

Log on to our website to register.

www.mebmaher.wixsite.com/website[2]

---

2. https://www.mebmaher.wixsite.com/website

Michael Maher Ministries

46 Penguin Road

Pringle Bay, 7196

South Africa

Phone: +27 082-974-3599

On the Web

<u>www.mebmaher.wixsite.com/website</u>[3]

---

3. http://www.mebmaher.wixsite.com/website

[1] https://en.wikipedia.org/wiki/Ishmaelites

[2] https://en.wikipedia.org/wiki/Edom

[3] https://en.wikipedia.org/wiki/Bar_Kokhba_revolt

[4] https://en.wikipedia.org/wiki/Timeline_of_the_Palestine_region

[5] https://www.worldometers.info/world-population/state-of-palestine-population/

[6] https://en.wikipedia.org/wiki/Palestinians_in_Jordan

[7] https://en.wikipedia.org/wiki/Origin_of_the_Palestinians

[8] https://en.wikipedia.org/wiki/Khitan_(circumcision)

[9] https://en.wikipedia.org/wiki/Edom#Conversion_to_Judaism

Don't miss out!

Visit the website below and you can sign up to receive emails whenever Michael Maher publishes a new book. There's no charge and no obligation.

https://books2read.com/r/B-A-BYNF-RRNVD

BOOKS2READ

Connecting independent readers to independent writers.

Did you love *Two Israels Unveiled*? Then you should read *Reign of the Anti-Christ*[4] by Michael E.B. Maher!

[5]

This book is written to explain what the bible teaches about the anti-Christ and his government. The apostle John is the one who specifically named this individual the "anti-Christ". Nevertheless the anti-Christ also has various other titles ascribed to him, i.e. the apostle John also refers to him as the beast and the apostle Paul refers to him as the man of sin, the son of perdition and the lawless one. So who is the anti-Christ? The bible reveals to us a very different person to most narratives about him that are in the public domain. In the book of Revelation John reveals to us that the number of the beast is 666, which he tell us is the number of a man. And so we know that the anti-Christ is a man. However although the anti-Christ is a man, we see in this book

---

4. https://books2read.com/u/m2Ear6

5. https://books2read.com/u/m2Ear6

that he is no ordinary man. This book explains where the anti-Christ originated from, where he is currently located and when the world can expect to see him appear. This book also discusses the key issue of the popular support that the anti-Christ will receive when he does appear and the reason for his popularity. And then finally this book explains the type and extent of government that the anti-Christ will set up in the earth, and how that government will impact the various people groups in the earth.

Read more at https://mebmaher.wixsite.com/website.

Also by Michael Maher

Israel's Prophetic Journey
Two Israels Unveiled

Watch for more at https://mebmaher.wixsite.com/website.

About the Author

From childhood, Michael E.B. Maher has always known that the Lord's call was upon his life for the ministry. When he was saved at the age of twenty-two, almost immediately the Lord Jesus began to deal with him about entering the ministry. However, it was only many years later that he committed to the Lord to answer the Lord's call to the ministry. And so, in 2014 Michael Maher Ministries was begun. From the beginning, the mandate given to Michael from the Lord Jesus was to preach the word. And so, this ministry preaches the word of God on every available platform around the world.

Read more at https://mebmaher.wixsite.com/website.